"This handy, readable guide shows nonprofit boards and staff that they can build a culture of sustainable philanthropic fundraising. The chapters cover 'the what and the why' of key elements for success while the embedded tale, 'The Magic Minds Story,' illustrates the 'how.'"

— TIM SEILER

Rosso Fellow in Philanthropic Studies;
Former Director of The Fund Raising School Indiana University Lilly Family School of Philanthropy

"Philanthropy and fundraising are part of our everyday lives, and are what makes our communities and organizations strong in the United States. Add to this the faith component, and you have the makings of even stronger and more successful results when seeking support for faith-based organizations. This book commendably illustrates the confluence of best practices with biblical and spiritual bases, and adroitly fills in the complete picture of how faith-based organizations should practice fundraising, while sharing practical as well as inspirational advice."

— LILYA WAGNER

Director, Philanthropic Service for Institutions;
Faculty Member, Lilly Family School of Philanthropy at Indiana University

"Jamie makes a strong case for a shift in focus from transactional to transformational as a multiplier of both impact and funding.

This shift in focus has turned our organization around and left others in our community and beyond asking for our secret. Its a joy to finally have Jamie's wisdom in a book to help let the 'cat(s)' out of the bag."

— DARLA JONES

Executive Director, Marsha's Place Pregnancy Resource Center

WHAT OTHERS ARE SAYING

"In over 25 years of fundraising experience I've never heard anyone enunciate more clearly how to build philanthropic sustainability in your organization. Working with Jamie and his team at JDLA as they helped us implement the ideas outlined in this book turned our whole organization around. From distracted and in debt to focused and funded, we watched our entire constituency grow deeper in their engagements with our vision and mission, as we stopped focusing on money and ourselves and started focusing on impact and others. If the sustainability of your cause matters to you this is the book that everyone on your staff and board need to read, discuss and implement."

— RICHARD KLOPP
CEO, Water for Good

"Every once in a while you are introduced to a person and the ideas they share with you are nothing short of revolutionary in your life. In fact, you know the moment you hear them if you will apply the principles they advocate, it's going to provide a powerful impact on the organization you have been pouring your blood, sweat, and tears into. And not only are these ideas going to multiply the current impact of your organization, but they are going to make it financially viable and sustainable far into the future.

Jamie Levy was just such a person as this to me and his revolutionary ideas are captured in this compelling book on philanthropy. The principles in this book really work and they will supercharge your philanthropic efforts regardless of whether you are a small start up charity or a large established organization."

— DAN SCHAFER
President, World Gospel Mission

PHILANTHROPY

$$Philanthropy = \heartsuit + \text{☺}$$

DISCOVER YOUR NONPROFIT'S
TRUE POTENTIAL

JAMIE LEVY

ISBN-13: 978-0692179536 (JDLevy & Associates)

JDLevy & Associates, Inc.
PMB 102
3557 N. Newton Street
Jasper, IN 47546

jdlevyassociates.com

My recognition and thanks go out to the numerous individuals who have helped me build my understanding in this great field. I give full acknowledgment to them all, whoever they may be, for laying the groundwork for development. I want to especially acknowledge The Fund Raising School (TFRS) and The Lilly School of Philanthropy (formerly the Center of Philanthropy) at Indiana University. I am a product of these great institutions, and the knowledge, teaching, and experience through them have shaped my approach and philosophy in the field. Furthering that I want to express my gratitude to the late Henry "Hank" Rosso and his work in providing a pathway we could all follow. He is a pioneer and legend in professionalizing the nonprofit sector and our understandings of fundraising. Through my work, teaching, and writing you can easily see the footprint of Hank, TFRS and The School of Philanthropy.

I want to specifically thank God, my wife, and my family. I want to extend a special thanks to my mentors, especially Dr. Lilya Wager, Dr. Tim Seiler, and Dr. Gene Temple. These three amazing individuals invested in me from an early place and shaped who I am. I am deeply grateful to them for their care as I have developed professionally over the years. My own insights have been greatly enhanced through my experiences of learning and teaching with them. This experience has been pivotal in fueling my thirst for knowledge and understanding.

Thank you all,

Jamie D. Levy
Jeremiah 33:3

P.S. - Special thanks to God, my family, the JDLA family, Darla Jones, and Jeremy Secrest.

CONTENTS

A NOTE FROM THE AUTHOR

I'm going to make four assumptions about you:
  1. *You have a passion to make the world a better place.*
  2. *You're already working to pursue that passion.*
  3. *The process for effective change can be confusing.*
  4. *You learn all you can to help make the world the best it can be.*

I'm also going to throw out an idea that goes along with those assumptions:

Most of us have an extremely limited perspective of what philanthropy is, and that hurts ourselves, our organizations, and the causes we're working toward impacting.

However, if we discover a bigger vision of philanthropy, we then can equip ourselves and our organizations to better discover and pursue that passion we hold so dearly. We'll be armed with resources to make a greater difference in our mission and society.

What is the cause you're passionate about? It may be the injustice of human trafficking, the fight against poverty, the need for a clear understanding of the gospel, unleashing the arts, educating the next generation, equipping marriages, or caring for orphans in a third-world country. Whatever the cause you are passionate about may be, we can often become overwhelmed at where to begin to make an impact.

The problem may seem so big that often our best efforts seem like a drop in the ocean. Then adding the reality of connecting people to the cause can seem like a person needs to resort to teeth-pulling, obligation, or manipulation just to keep the lights on. Despite these efforts, you also wonder whether you're working to just bring money in the door or you're creating value for your cause.

There must be a better way. I believe there is, and this book can help.

My insights are formed through various means. They are informed through my relationship with Christ and my understanding of what love is as expressed through philanthropy. Insights have developed from working with hundreds of nonprofits for more than 20 years to date, learning and studying at the best institutions in the field and training tens of thousands of professionals. Through these opportunities, I have discovered insights that can help the organization you're passionate about make a difference.

While the study of philanthropy is a very robust and often complex field, this book distills core concepts to help you and your organization work more effectively. It will aid in mobilizing the community and building long-term sustainability around your mission and vision by equipping people to become advocates of the cause—advocates representing those who will stand in the gap for the individuals you serve.

Think of it as boarding an airplane to fly at a 30,000-foot view over philanthropy to answer three basic questions:

1. *What is philanthropy really?*
2. *How does it work?*
3. *Why can a true understanding of it transform your nonprofit (and the world)?*

Buckle your seatbelt as we prepare for departure.

Jamie

THE
CHARITABLE
SECTOR

"The place God calls you to is the place where your deep gladness and the world's deep hunger meet."

- Frederick Buechner

Of the thousands of questions nonprofits ask my team and me, two questions climb their way to the top:

1. *How can my nonprofit raise more money?*
2. *How can we create long-term sustainability?*

While nearly every organization in the charitable (nonprofit) sector bring up these questions, they are sometimes answered without a real context of what the answers should be. I'd like to challenge you to think of your mission or organization in a larger context than just raising or sustaining funds.

Your work and organization are part of the charitable sector. This means you're in a different part of the economy from business or government. It's easy for nonprofits to view themselves with poor self-esteem because they are not turning a profit and don't have government-size budgets. When we look at the bigger picture, however, you might be surprised by the potential for influence you have.

Here are some interesting facts based on historical data:

- *The charitable sector includes nearly 1.6 million tax-exempt (nonprofit) organizations.[1]*
- *Charitable sector revenue includes nearly $1.4 trillion.[1]*
- *The charitable sector's share of Gross Domestic Product is 2.1%.[2]*
- *Nonprofits account for 10% of all wages and salaries paid in the United States.[3]*
- *In 1904, there were only 138 registered nonprofit organizations.[4]*
- *Nonprofit volunteers provide more than 8 billion hours of service time, creating more than $193 billion in economic value.[5]*
- *Foundations, through their grants, produce more than 500,000 jobs annually.[6]*
- *Giving makes us healthier.[7]*
- *Giving makes us happier.[8]*

$$Philanthropy = \heartsuit + \text{☺}$$

Raising the funds to meet your budget doesn't seem as overwhelming now, does it?

Frederick Buechner, a writer and theologian, said, "The place God calls you to is the place where your deep gladness and the world's deep hunger meet."

This is a great description of what philanthropy and the charitable sector are all about. Philanthropy is the place where passion, love, societal need, and transformation come together. It serves both the needs of those who utilize the services of an organization and the needs of supporters to express their purpose and passions. Philanthropy can be the glue of society, bringing together the "deep gladness" of a supporter and the "deep hunger" of someone's need.

Philanthropy = ♡ + 🧍

THE MAGIC MINDS STORY
Beginning

Meet Charlie. Charlie is a professional illusionist who has a heart to teach magic tricks to under-resourced children. If you ask him, he'll say "Learning magic is magic to your mind." In other words, the very task of learning how to do sleight of hand, misdirection, and how people perceive things provides great life skills to a person. "Illusion isn't magic, it's art," he says. Charlie wants to provide children who might gravitate toward illusion and creative thinking the opportunity to learn it and reap the rewards of increased people skills, learning ability, and creativity.

Charlie began a nonprofit, Magic Minds, a few years ago to bring these lessons into local schools to ultimately see under-resourced children understand and embrace creativity and pursue careers in creative fields.

A nonprofit organization is a matchmaker of sorts. Understanding and operating out of this perspective can tremendously elevate the value of the work the organization does. You are not a beggar. You are not an obligation. You are an invitation for someone to connect with their passion or "gladness."

A business operates on an exchange. The coffee shop makes a fantastic Caffe' Americano, and you pay $4 for it. You exchange money for coffee. Both sides win.

Too often we think of a nonprofit as a one-way transaction. We merely ask people to give. When we consider donors or volunteers as merely a commodity to be used, we revert to a one-way transaction perspective. When we operate out of that perspective, we rob ourselves and our supporters of the full benefit our services provide.

We can instead create a relationship and discover the heart of our supporters. When we look for ways our organization and the donor's heart intersect, we are operating in a mutual exchange of values and allowing passions to be realized.

Philanthropy = ♡ + 🧍

THE MAGIC MINDS STORY
Serving both sides

Over time, as Charlie naturally shared what he was working on with his illusionist friends, many of them expressed an interest in helping. Charlie barely had to ask.

One of his friend said, "I love it! I can use my magic skills and passion to help someone."

Charlie began to realize his nonprofit wasn't just serving the children; it was also serving his friends by giving them an outlet to use their skills and passion.

Let's revisit our big questions of raising money and creating long-term sustainability. When we overlook what motivates supporters to become involved, ignore what they seek to receive from participating, and don't understand the exchange of value we create, we miss critical elements of how to raise funds and create sustainability.

This exchange of value is the basis of sustainable fundraising and the essence of public charity. A nonprofit is designed to lose money when performing its main mission-focused service. This service creates value to society, but the organization cannot continue providing the service without funding, relationships, and renewal, which come from other sources. By necessity and design, fundraising and community support are the lifeblood of a nonprofit organization. They are not a byproduct or necessary evil; they are the life of the charitable organization.

The questions of "How can we raise more money?" and "How do we create long-term sustainability?" are not the right questions to start with. Instead, let's begin with these two questions:

  1. *How can we better engage those who care?*
  2. *How do we build life advocates for our cause?*

When we engage those who care about our organization's cause, by working together to fulfill its mission and pursue a vision bigger than ourselves, the money will follow.

Philanthropy = ♡ + 🙂

In the same way, long-term sustainability is about more than having enough funds to keep the lights on. Sustainability is developing ongoing and deepening community mobilization, impact, and renewal around a cause or movement. If these things are happening, revenue will naturally follow.

Why?

Money is only one piece of the value exchanged. It's often a "trailing edge" exchange as well. This means money follows once other pieces of value have been provided, not before. Money comes after things like a relationship and passion have already been established. Money in the door on a certain date is a result of things done two, three, five, or more years ago—not yesterday.

You might say, "This sounds like a nice theory, but is it actually effective in the real world?"

This philosophy has been developed over years of extensive experience and revelation in the charitable sector and through formal education and research. My colleagues include faculty members at the IU Center and School of Philanthropy, School of Public and Environmental Affairs, and The Fund Raising School. My firm, JDLevy & Associates (JDLA), has trained more than 30,000 professionals from some 30 countries. We have worked with hundreds upon hundreds of nonprofit organizations and non-governmental organizations. The focus of JDLA is on organizational development as it pertains to philanthropic sustainability.

$$Philanthropy = \heartsuit + \text{☺}$$

This work allows my team and me the privilege to work with thousands of donors, board members, staff, and volunteers as well. Their insight and experiences have proven to us the power of true philanthropy. It can and does change the way an organization operates and how it impacts its corner of the world.

$$Philanthropy = \heartsuit + \text{☺}$$

Charlie soon had a small army of illusionists, both amateur and professional, who joined in his cause. As the work grew, Charlie realized he needed additional funds for supplies and basic operating costs. Charlie began personally sharing the needs with his group of illusionists. Individual members gave toward the project, and others put on a variety of magic shows as fundraisers. They were able to fund the necessary supplies and costs.

The strong relationship Charlie had with his illusionist friends fueled their desire to get involved. They knew and trusted Charlie. They believed in the work.

CHAPTER 2

WHAT IS PHILANTHROPY?

Philanthropy empowers transformation through relationships

Philanthropy literally means "love of man or humanity."

It comes from the Greek root words "philos" and "philein," meaning, "loving" and "to love." "Anthro" comes from the Greek word for "humanity" or "man." Love of humankind. When we see philanthropy as it was first expressed by God, we begin to glimpse how powerful it can be. God created mankind in love. In John 3:16, we read "For God so loved the world that he gave his one and only Son, that whoever believes in him shall not perish but have eternal life." God gave everything out of love to us. Out of this love, we are equipped to love and connect people to their calling around passions and causes to transform the world.

Many have misunderstood philanthropy to be a transactional pursuit of money instead of an outlet for people to express their passion. A place where civil society can invest in what society holds dear. Rather than helping people understand the truest purpose of the organization's cause and inviting them to deeply invest themselves in a greater purpose, we've lessened it by using guilt, coercion, or influence to raise funds. Often the focus is on begging and seeing people as a commodity to be won by trying to sell them on a quick gift to fix a certain current issue as opposed to engaging them in holistic relationships. When in a true philanthropic setting, we are engaging individuals at a heart level—the movement from token to sacrifice in how we give. There is often a disposable attitude toward the donor and volunteer as opposed to building life-relationships that can become generational.

Philanthropy operates and expresses itself in the charitable (nonprofit) sector.

$$Philanthropy = \heartsuit + \text{☺}$$

Most people think of philanthropy as large charitable donations by the wealthy. Yet look at these surprising statistics:

- *The large majority of the U.S. population gives and volunteers their time with charitable causes.*[1]
- *The more families earn, the larger the gifts, but the smaller percentage of income they give. For the families who earn less, they give higher percentages of incomes to charity.*[2]

Philanthropy isn't reserved for the wealthy.

So then, what is philanthropy...really?

Philanthropy begins with a foundation of Scripture.

God himself, who is love, committed the first philanthropic act. God's creation of the Earth, its workings, and its plant and animal forms of life is detailed in the Bible in the first 26 verses of Genesis. After He creates, God pronounces the thing "good," meaning valuable. These verses also point out the renewal of each created thing: each day turns to night and becomes another day (Gen. 1:5); plants, trees, and fruit are created with seeds to reproduce (Gen. 1:11); and creatures are told to multiply (Gen. 1:22).[3]

The only thing left to create was a way through which God's valuable, renewable creation could be used. We are told God said, "Let us make mankind in our own image, in our likeness..." (Gen. 1:26). "Us" refers to God the Father, the Son, and the Holy Spirit, also known as the Trinity. God engaged in philanthropy through giving of Himself, His Son, and His Spirit in creation. God intended the same relational unity experienced by the Trinity to happen between humankind, His ultimate creation. In the book of John,

Philanthropy = ♡ + 🙂

God reveals why—because He "so loved" what He had created, He ultimately gave Himself (John 3:16).

How did God intend for that unity and expression of His love to occur? Through people caring about other people. God has called us to love others as He loves us.

Throughout history we see this love of man expressed. From parents adopting an orphan to the founding of universities to a musician creating beautiful music to the abolition of slavery to someone mowing their neighbor's lawn to the establishment of hospitals, the love of man is seen in big and small ways in all areas of life.

The Three Pillars

One challenge we have in life is knowing how to connect ourselves to opportunities to love others. Philanthropy serves as that connection. Philanthropy provides structure to help us express this love to other people.

Philanthropy is expressed in society in three core ways. We call these voluntary expressions of love - the three pillars of true philanthropy:

1. **Giving of Giftedness:** *Freely giving our own time and giftedness/talents to God's purpose.*
2. **Giving of Treasure:** *The act of sharing God's resources through us, as He owns it all.*
3. **Giving of Spirit:** *Advocacy, intercession, championing something we value as much or more than ourselves, connecting others to the cause, and coming alongside those we care for.*

Philanthropy = ♡ + ☺

Volunteering, giving, and advocating allow us to connect more deeply with what we care about. The highest level of this allows us to fully express and align our values with a cause that we're passionate about and called into.

Nonprofit organizations uniquely engage with all three pillars. Government and business cannot work with all three. Nonprofits exist to provide the public good by engaging donors, volunteers, and advocates in a cause they share, ultimately creating a renewal in community.

$$Philanthropy = \heartsuit + \text{☺}$$

THE MAGIC MINDS STORY
Sharing the vision

As a professional, Charlie knew the illusion business. He knew there was no practical way to turn a profit teaching magic to under-resourced children. He also knew the government wasn't going to be starting a department of illusion anytime soon, which was why he formed Magic Minds a few years ago.

As Magic Minds began to grow, Charlie's vision grew to expand its services into counties surrounding his. Yet to do that required more funds and more time than he or his group could provide.

What they could provide, though, was advocacy. These illusionists began sharing the vision of Magic Minds with their friends and colleagues. They shared their experiences and the growth seen in the kids they worked with, and they shared with people how they could get involved. Pretty soon, additional illusionists were signing up to help, and even "non-magic" people began giving toward this compelling work.

How is philanthropy transformational?

Philanthropy does not just enable us to meet a need; it empowers change.

It empowers change in three ways:

1. *It meets the needs of those being served through our organization.*
2. *It meets the needs of meaning, purpose, and expression of values for supporters.*
3. *It provides an opportunity to be life giving to all it touches by allowing those who care and share to discover their calling and pursue their highest potential.*

Ultimately, it empowers transformation through relationships.

The transformation is both the change in the cause we're working toward and the change in the life of the supporter who engages with the work. The supporter's highest potential is reached when the individual finds they can more fully discover their calling by giving of themselves through investing their resources, time, and heart into something they deeply value.

Think about the effect on your cause, your community, and the world not only if needs are being met by your nonprofit; but also if those who support your work are able to discover and grow their passions and giftings. As people step more fully into who God designed them to be, they begin to find the place where their deep gladness and the world's deep hunger meet. That's the powerful privilege, responsibility, and opportunity of a nonprofit organization.

Philanthropy = ♡ + 🙂

When we limit philanthropy to merely money, we don't allow change to occur in society. This is transactional philanthropy. Transactional philanthropy isn't philanthropy at all. Just as God's love for man isn't limited to money, an organization's love for man can't be limited to money.

Philanthropy becomes transformational when we understand, embrace, and live out all three pillars.

$$Philanthropy = \heartsuit + \text{👤}$$

THE MAGIC MINDS STORY
Transformation

As more people got involved with Magic Minds, they began to bring ideas to Charlie on how to more effectively serve the children.

"What if we brought two illusionists to each classroom? Then more children would get individual attention and opportunities to work with the supplies."

"If we left instruction sheets with each class, kids could practice card tricks on their own at home."

"What if we offered a scholarship for an outstanding young illusionist that sent them to magic camp for a week in the summer, all expenses paid?"

Not only was Charlie bringing people on board to serve the mission and vision he presented, but they were making the work better. Their ideas yielded greater impact in the lives of students than Charlie could do or think on his own. Transformation was happening.

For the bottom-line focused of us (you know who you are), like we mentioned earlier, the exciting by-product of practicing all three pillars of philanthropy is that the funds you need tend to follow.

Did you know 80 to 90% of all individual donors in the United States are volunteers? Donors who also volunteer generally

- *give the highest average gifts,*
- *give the highest annual gifts,*
- *have the longest donor relationship with charities they value,*
- *are the most loyal,*
- *are the most likely to make a planned giving decision, and*
- *are more empowered as advocates for the cause.*

When we begin to see a supporter as someone whom we are helping discover their passions and giftings, we begin to discover what love of man is about. We begin to catalyze real community change and transformation.

A donor gave $500 to a local Salvation Army in Southern Indiana. It was her first gift to the organization. The Executive Director called to thank her and asked about her desires, passion, interest, and how the organization could help facilitate those needs. The Executive Director had to stop what she was doing, prioritize her time to meet the donor where she was, and explore how to foster the donor's potential. Soon after, the organization was surprised to receive a $10,000 donation from the donor with a card mentioning how much she appreciated the time and their interest in her. When we practice true philanthropy, the money follows.

Philanthropy = ♡ *+* 👤

When we move away from transactions, we break through barriers and begin a new focus on authentic relationships. The donor and volunteer become partners of the organization. Together, we grow and empower one another to create change through exchanging values. This begins to create a culture of philanthropy that unifies a group that cares about the same larger cause. When people find that place of meaning, they change society.

THE CHARITABLE SECTOR AND PHILANTHROPY:

HOW DOES IT WORK?

The highest purpose of a nonprofit organization is to act for the good of others—the community served by the organization.

Why is there a charitable (nonprofit) sector?

Nonprofit organizations provide services that promote the public good. They are a platform that allows society to discover some of its greatest passions, to glue the economy together, and to create community transformation. As mentioned earlier, nonprofit organizations fill a gap in society that government cannot meet and that business typically cannot make a profit and/or do with same quality and trust from society. A nonprofit typically provides services at a monetary loss.

For example, Magic Minds does not charge for their services. If there was a way to turn a profit teaching magic to under-resourced children, then an entrepreneurial illusionist would create a business around that idea. Charlie, a professional illusionist, knew this wouldn't work financially. The design of a nonprofit to lose money through its main services is not a bad thing; it's simply how the organization operates.

The charitable sector is bound by a unique dynamic of mission statements, clients, donors, grants, government, and non-distribution constraints.

Philanthropy = ♡ + ☺

Where did the formal charitable sector come from?

Here is a quick history of the charitable sector:

- *The Revenue Act of 1894 established incentives to have defined, formal volunteer boards with tax-exempt status for nonprofits.*
- *The Revenue Act of 1954 established Section 501c(3) of the Internal Revenue Code (the designation for a tax-exempt charitable organization) and gave certain responsibilities to board members.*
- *The Not-for-Profit Organizing Act of 1971 defined the board as the core group of individuals responsible for the organization and provided formal guidelines for nonprofit boards.*

Nonprofits now serve society in the form of charities, foundations, social welfare organizations, and professional and trade organizations in 28 different classifications ranging from cemeteries to trusts to service providers.

What is a nonprofit organization, and how does it operate?

A nonprofit is formed when a group of people believe a need exists and when there is a gap that keeps this need from being met by business or government. A group of individuals then form a charitable nonprofit organization to fill the gap. This is like the gap Charlie noticed in teaching magic to under-resourced children. The illusionists captured the vision of what should be and discussed how to create change around the need of the people they were helping. He believed magic was the vehicle that could help children learn increased people skills, social learning, and creativity. The issue was not magic; it was what he saw the children were missing, and magic was the vehicle for change.

Philanthropy = ♡ + ☺

A nonprofit is driven by a "mission and service bottom line" instead of a financial bottom line. Since it loses money by design, the loss must be covered by other means like earned income, fee-for-service, endowment revenue, grants, service fees, government funding, and philanthropic fundraising. For example, because Magic Minds' services were free, their expenses had to be covered by donations and fundraisers.

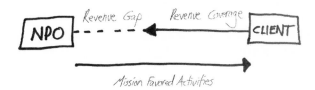

Revenue Gap: *Donors provide value through financial support, volunteering, leveraging networks, insight, advocacy, and championing the cause.*

Service Provision: *The organization provides value through social investment opportunities, recognition, opportunities for involvement, and responsible stewardship of gifts.*

Leadership of nonprofit organizations

Despite the varying types of nonprofit organizations, all share one thing in common. By law, every nonprofit is governed by a board of directors (or regents, trustees, governors, elders, etc.).

The board is the single most important group of any nonprofit organization. They are the most closely involved with donors and volunteers. Not only are they legally responsible for the organization, but they are socially responsible for being good stewards of the organization's resources. They must make sure the organization's mission is fulfilled and that it operates as a trustworthy and effective steward of the resources entrusted to it by donors. Technically, the community "owns" the organization, and the board serves at the will of the "donor." The board is the most in-depth, legally charged advocates for the cause.

The highest purpose of a nonprofit organization is to act for the good of others—the community served by the organization. The nonprofit becomes the voice of those they serve. In other words, it is the board's responsibility to safeguard the public good. To accomplish this, a board must consist of committed individuals who fully understand their roles and obligations and who share a passion for the cause. Board members must also function as a cohesive unit. They are a body of leadership that serves, governs, and leads the organization toward the achievement of its mission. The board and its members, by law, are held accountable for the actions and inactions of the organization. They are proportionately liable for any wrongdoing in the organization. To help establish accountability, a board and its members should continually evaluate the results of its mission,

Philanthropy = ♡ + 🙂

stewardship, and leadership. The bottom line is the board is extremely important.

Given the importance of the board, it's interesting that a board member of General Electric can be paid $8,500 per hour, while a board member of a nonprofit, who makes decisions that affect the daily lives of families and individuals, serves as a volunteer and often serves without a proper understanding of their role. Many times, board members of nonprofits find themselves serving as an obligation and often do not know what success is or how they can add value to the cause. Unfortunately, board members may not have life-enriching experiences that help connect them to their potential and move deeper into their own calling for a cause. Philanthropy changes this by providing a way to engage people holistically in their calling in society. It gives them a means to engage their resources, their giftedness, and their spirit to create positive impact on lives around them. In Chapter 5, we will explore this topic more fully.

CHAPTER 4

THE THREE PILLARS:

A DEEPER LOOK AT PHILANTHROPY'S VALUE

Organizations are a vehicle for donors to connect with and act on their love for humankind.

Why this matters to your organization

If we had a pop quiz right now and I asked you, "What is philanthropy?" some people might say it is a mutual fund or the study of a guy named Phil. However, you could sum it up by saying, "Philanthropy simply means the love of mankind."

If you wanted to get bonus points, you could then add these statements:

- *Philanthropy is connecting someone's time, resources, and spirit to a cause they're passionate about.*
- *This is seen in the three pillars of philanthropy: volunteering, giving, and advocacy.*

Finally, if you were going for a gold star, you could define the three pillars:

- *Volunteering is freely giving of ourselves to what we care about.*
- *Giving is society investing its resources in what it values.*
- *Advocacy is interceding (or giving of our heart) in support of shared vision and values for something greater than ourselves.*

For us to adequately discuss fundraising and sustainability, we need to unpack these ideas further.

Philanthropy springs from love, which is a free choice. Completely voluntary. Meaning if you love cats, you'll spend your time, resources, and heart to care for cats. If I love dogs and try to convert you into loving dogs, you may go along for a little while out of kindness. However, if you don't truly love dogs, your heart for dogs is not going to grow, and I'll end up becoming a nuisance to you, as I invite you to care about dogs. You love cats.

$$Philanthropy = \heartsuit + \text{\Large ☺}$$

On the other hand, if we both love cats, then we share the same value and vision. You and I will both freely choose to invest ourselves in caring for cats. We don't need to be obligated or coerced. It will naturally spring out of our hearts. As we invest together, we'll discover a growing understanding and passion for cats. We'll have a growing desire to care for cats and will be looking for an outlet to express that desire. We want someone to connect us to the cause.

Therefore, philanthropy involves an exchange of values. The charitable sector, where nonprofits operate, becomes the outlet for this exchange to happen in a way that government and business simply cannot operate. Nonprofits are the vehicle for connecting people with common passions, like cats, and allowing those individuals the opportunity to express their passion by connecting their time (volunteering), resources (giving), and hearts (advocacy).

These three pillars work together to form the holistic expression of philanthropy through transformational relationships.

$$Philanthropy = \heartsuit + \text{⚲}$$

FIRST PILLAR: *GIVING*

A deeper look at giving in the United States

The average U.S. nonprofit's fundraising program will lose more new donors in the first year of donor giving than it retains. In addition, for every new dollar the organization acquires, the organization will lose a dollar by year end.

Why? The number-one reason donors stop giving is indifference. Donors feel the organization is indifferent toward their relationship. Donors feel the organization looks at them as a checkbook and nothing more.

Yet would that donor stop loving cats? No! If you're a cat lover, you'll just find a new place to love cats. The nonprofit organization is not the goal; it's the vehicle. The cause is the goal. You'll find a way to love cats through a different organization.

$$Philanthropy = \heartsuit + \text{🙂}$$

Let's look at some interesting historical statistics about giving:

- *To date, the approximate revenue of all nonprofit organizations is $1.7 trillion.[1]*
- *$390 billion of that comes from individuals, corporations, and foundations.[2]*
- *$337 billion (86%) comes from individuals (including $25 billion from family foundations and also added in is estate and planned giving from individuals).[1]*
- *Giving has increased every year since 1977, except a small decline in 1987 and 2008-2009.[3]*
- *As a family makes less, they give higher and higher percentages of income to charity.[4, 5, 6]*
- *Even during the Great Recession, the total drop in real dollars was less than 3%, and of that drop, less than 1% was in individual donor behavior.[7]*
- *Americans give approximately 2% of their income to charity.[7]*
- *Research shows giving makes us happier and those who give are healthier overall.[8]*
- *Women give 156% more than men of the same age and income.[8]*
- *Approximately 89% of all donors are people of faith (claim to attend one religious service or more per month).[9]*
- *Volunteering drives giving. It is about connection. Volunteering increases connection and the more people connection, the more they give.*

Donors tend to give at the same overall monetary levels during a recession, within a few percentage points. However, one area affected is the number of organizations a donor will give to. The person giving to 10 organizations will now give to five. If the donor narrows the number of organizations donated to, what influences their decision? Donors will choose organizations they have a relationship with—the ones where they're connected and advocating for the cause. When donors choose, relationships drive their decisions.

$$Philanthropy = \heartsuit + \text{☺}$$

For example, as the recession began to hit in the summer of 2007, the first organizations to take a hit were direct inner-city service organizations. The practical reason behind this is because these organizations typically have the least developed fundraising infrastructure compared to other nonprofits. They often don't have the systems or a prioritized focus to engage donors relationally. When donors decide to prioritize, even if they see value in the cause, they'll stop giving if they don't have a relationship to the organization.

The "Right" Donors

If your nonprofit serves cats and you have many sacrificial donors connected to your organization, a crucial thing happens: these donors get involved and get other cat lovers connected to the cause. A typical cat donor may give only $5 but brings seven of her cat-loving friends to partner in the cause. An existing donor's ability to open the door to new relationships with others who share a passion for the organization's cause is the greatest asset the right donor can bring to your organization. Sacrificial donors build a movement around your cause.

Finding the right people to connect to your organization is critical. A shotgun approach to the community is not the answer. Being strategic, based on relationships and interest, is the key. Existing and committed donor relationships have an innate ability to find people who connect with the nonprofit's cause. When the organization's focus is on maintaining and enabling relationships with the right people, these sacrificial donors seek to make a difference.

Movements and community transformation don't happen through a few "elite" individuals; they happen through an army of "average" people.

$$Philanthropy = \heartsuit + \text{☺}$$

SECOND PILLAR: *VOLUNTEERING*

Connecting volunteers to your nonprofit not only provides a practical way to support and sustain your organization's services but also provides credibility and confidence regarding stewardship of donor resources. I often hear donors say, "If an organization is engaging that much volunteer time, I know my dollar is going further here than at another organization." Donors see more impact with the gifts they give when volunteers are engaged. Donors see more relationships moving forward the cause.

The value of one hour of volunteer time is more than $24. Based on that rate and the number of volunteers in the U.S., volunteers provide almost $275 billion in labor value to our economy. This equals about 9 million full-time employees.

As the impact of volunteers to your organization is extremely high, it's important to value, recognize, and track volunteer engagement. I once was in an organization that worked through more than 3,000 volunteers. Those volunteers added the equivalent of nearly $3 million worth of labor value to the cause each year. In the 50-year history of the organization, the labor value was never included in the budgeting process. For example, we would say, "We can serve 60,000 people for X dollars." Yet we were incapable of serving that many people at that cost without the tremendous impact of volunteer labor.

We finally came to realize our budget to serve 60,000 people was not just X dollars; it also included the nearly $3 million worth of volunteer hours. Once we understood this, it changed the behavior of our organization. We connected the value of volunteer work to the overall resources needed to accomplish the mission.

$$Philanthropy = \heartsuit + \text{☺}$$

As organizations, it therefore makes sense to prioritize and invest the necessary resources to create systems to collect and analyze the contributions of volunteer work. We also need to recognize and value our relationships with volunteers because that is part of deepening their connection to our organization and building them into lifelong donors and advocates. When volunteers are connected to the cause, they build the movement.

THIRD PILLAR: *ADVOCACY*

The greatest nonprofit movements were not created by twisting people's arms to give financially to a cause they didn't have a heart for. Some of the greatest movements centered on organizations mobilizing advocates to be a change for their cause. These movements gave advocates an opportunity to share their heart for the cause with other like-minded people. These individuals embraced, promoted, and championed values they cared about. Advocates were able to help others understand the organization's values, vision, and mission. Advocates were empowered to make a change for the organization's cause.

When we help people find their deepest meaning in our cause, they begin to stand in the gap with us, share our work with others, and make change happen in the cause they care about. Their passion becomes both strategic and contagious. Someone becoming an advocate is the capstone of building relationships through philanthropy.

Since we are passionate about our cause, it's tempting to believe everyone else should care about it as well. We share the need, the solution, and the vision. It's what we do. It's even who we are. We do that to light the fires of those who

Philanthropy = ♡ + ☺

share the same heart as we do. We're on a mission to ignite those who are passionate about the same cause as us.

However, not everyone shares this cause, and that is okay. When we spend our time guilting and obligating people to give toward a cause they do not share passion for, we limit our opportunities to create genuine advocates for the cause. Those who don't share the passion will not share it with others. Sure, they can still give. Of course, they can still make a difference. But those donors are not who we should be investing our highest resources into, even if they have the largest checkbooks. We must ensure we don't turn them into a commodity.

When we build relationships with like-minded people, we then need to empower those individuals to make change. We partner with advocates to help them find their greatest place of meaningful contribution to our cause and not just our largest need as an organization. Many organizations don't see much advocacy among their donors and volunteers because these individuals are not given the opportunity to get more engaged in the organization. However, when donors are given deepened exposure to an organization's mission through volunteering and giving, they will naturally connect other like-minded people to the organization.

$$Philanthropy = \heartsuit + \text{☺}$$

THE MAGIC MINDS STORY
Persuasion or invitation?

With the combined increase in vision and donors, Magic Minds was growing faster than Charlie ever anticipated. Charlie and the board decided to lease a facility to run the operations of their organization. The facility was modest but was still a significant financial responsibility based on their budget. It was a risk, but their current growth and plans to expand development made it a calculated risk.

Charlie's plan to expand development was to move beyond illusionists to successful business executives in the area. "Illusionists don't have money; executives do," thought Charlie. "This is a no-brainer."

However, Charlie encountered a whole new world. What had typically been a cause that "sells itself" became very difficult to connect with non-illusionists. Business executives respected the program. They congratulated him on the work. Some even gave small gifts. But only a few of the executives got involved or excited about the work.

Charlie ran reports and realized he raised fewer funds for Magic Minds from executives than from his middle-class illusionist friends. Though frustrated, Charlie began to discover the difference between persuasion and inviting an individual into a mission they already resonate with.

Each of these three pillars of philanthropy is rooted in the importance of the donor and volunteer relationship with the cause. A culture of philanthropy will focus on empowering all who share the vision and values of the cause to move toward their greatest potential for the cause.

The potential might look as unique as each person involved. It might be an exceptional relationship a volunteer has with local businesses to provide produce for a food co-op. It might be a local musician performing a benefit concert. It might be a senior praying for specific organizational needs. Each relationship is seen as unique. The person is seen as an asset partnering with the organization. It's a win-win relationship.

Organizations must begin to see themselves as a vehicle for the donors to connect with and act on their love for humankind. We seek to build a holistic relationship with our supporters to engage their greatest potential in the vision and values we share. That perspective is the foundation to a culture of philanthropy.

Philanthropy = ♡ + ☺

CHAPTER 5

A CULTURE OF PHILANTHROPY

Their roles move from knocking on doors to inviting people into something bigger than themselves.

What creates an organization's culture?

A culture is created through its values, traditions, symbols, attitudes, and beliefs. The culture unites everyone from staff to supporter. The board, staff, and volunteers embody, support, and celebrate the culture. Just like cultures of certain countries, cities, or communities, an organization's culture attracts people to take part and contribute to it. Culture is one of the strongest assets to an organization. As one saying puts it, "Culture eats strategy for lunch!"

A culture of philanthropy unifies a group of people who care about the same cause. It creates stronger advocates for the cause and encourages individuals to step into their greatest potential to love people through that cause. These are both the focus and the results of a healthy culture of philanthropy.

One of the first steps toward developing a healthy culture of philanthropy is to step back from looking at fundraising as a "necessary evil." Rather, see fundraising as a front door for relationships and mobilization. Begin seeing fundraising as a servant of philanthropy—a vehicle that allows society to invest in a shared vision and values. Like we mentioned earlier, relationships are centered on the cause and the value the donor and organization bring to one another.

Philanthropy = ♡ + ☺

Use these questions to help you begin evaluating your culture:

- *Does your organization view donors and volunteers as relationships to be invested in or as a nuisance to your work?*
- *Does your organization view donors as 30-year relationships or three-year commodities?*
- *Is your organization building a culture of mutual value and long-term relationships or short-term token gifts and transactions?*
- *Does your organization see donors and volunteers as advocates who can transform your organization and the community around them?*
- *Does your organization see the staff and board as the strongest partners and closest relationships, who need to be invested in to become true advocates for the cause?*
- *Does your organization view its job as helping individuals who share the cause's vision and values find their greatest potential in creating value and impact around the cause?*

Relationship Renewal

Harvard has a more than $34 billion endowment. Yes, billion. Harvard has the capacity to give full-ride scholarships into infinity, continue to grow every year, and never need to raise more money. It sounds like the ultimate dream for every nonprofit, doesn't it?

Yet Harvard also has one of the most robust and effective fundraising programs in the country. Why? Especially considering they are often criticized for "taking" money that could instead go to rescue missions or other organizations.

How do they rationalize that?

Philanthropy = ♡ + 🙂

Harvard's president gave a fascinating response, and I will paraphrase the interview conducted. He said, "You clearly don't understand what makes this institution Harvard. If we stop engaging the people who care about Harvard with the thing they care about, this institution will die because it's that very engagement that has made Harvard what it is."

That's powerful. The president of Harvard says it's not about their fundraising program or an endowment. It's about philanthropy; it's about relationships that transform. In the end, philanthropy and fundraising are not about money. They are about the exponential power between people with shared values coming together around a common cause. This power creates something more together than any one person could achieve alone.

When done correctly, fundraising creates a sustainable, renewable relationship between an organization and a donor. Fundraising can become a source of sustainability and organizational renewal because it forces a nonprofit to continually evaluate its relationship with donors, and donors' relationships with each other, to strengthen unity around the cause.

$$Philanthropy = \heartsuit + \text{☺}$$

The graphic below illustrates an ideal renewal process between the organization and donor as two equal parties. As their relationship progresses, they experience the following:

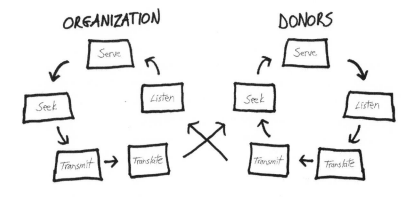

- **Seeking:** *Deepening understanding of the cause and its needs.*
- **Serving:** *Identifying ways to participate in the cause, educate, and deepen understanding of the need.*
- **Listening:** *Listening to perspectives, needs, and insights around the cause.*
- **Translating:** *Determining what is meaningful and applying it to the next level of relationship development.*
- **Transmitting:** *Acting upon the information gathered to better meet needs.*

Philanthropy = ♡ + 🙂

What does this relationship look like in "real time"?

We identify a donor relationship when we seek who shares an interest and connection to our cause. These two key findings should drive donor development. We must seek to understand donors before we can serve them. After serving donors through information, education, and inspiration around our shared cause, we listen. This listening involves asking for a donor's insight, striving to understand their needs and desires, and learning what the donor sees in our cause and organization. From here, we begin translating those insights into our relationship based on what we learned from the donor. We then transmit those insights through the activities of our relationships to strengthen the cause.

The same process continues through everyone involved in the organization, from staff to board members. We seek insights from them, serve them through engagement, listen to them, translate what we learn, and transmit it back into our organization.

We ask simple questions like

- *How are we doing?*
- *What do we need to better understand?*
- *What needs to be refined?*

We listen and then serve with the insight gained. We make changes, refine policies, strengthen services, and/or add new ones.

$$Philanthropy = \heartsuit + \text{☺}$$

When our focus is on the donor and volunteer, all feedback, good or bad, is useful to deepen donor relationships. The organization may discern new needs that fit the gifts and passions of certain donors. You may find a new service you added allows an individual donor to approach a business or foundation that funds that specific activity. The feedback opens the door to bring donors into a closer relationship with you.

When done correctly, the organization and donor relationship will renew and deepen itself. When done in a transactional manner, this relationship is one-sided and may not be sustained. Each cycle of seeking, serving, listening, translating, and transmitting is an opportunity to deepen the relationship. If it is maintained properly, the cycle never stops. If the cycle stops, the organization loses its unifying passion with donors, and relationships either stagnate or die entirely. Death does not necessarily mean the organization will close, but the relationship stops renewing the cause and inspiring change.

The strength of these healthy relationships allows organizations to evolve and renew. This renewal is why we call it transformational philanthropy. The relationships based around a common cause continually transform both the cause and the donor.

$$Philanthropy = \heartsuit + \text{☺}$$

THE MAGIC MINDS STORY
"That's pretty special."

After the struggle with getting "non-magic" people connected (some jokingly referred to them as "Muggles"), Charlie and the board began an intentional focus to search for other like-minded illusionists. Instead of advertising, they decided to meet with as many of the illusionist donors and volunteers as they could. They asked these donors and volunteers why they got connected, discussed ideas for improvement, and updated them on what Magic Minds had recently accomplished.

As they met with each person, Charlie and the board discovered passionate people who enjoyed using their illusion talents and interests to make a difference in the lives of others. One volunteer said, "Getting to know you all reminds me of why I got involved in the first place. I know I'm part of the team and not just a cog in the machine. It doesn't feel like I'm in a sales pitch but feels like I'm in a brainstorm meeting on how to help these kids by teaching them illusion. That's pretty special."

Transformational relationships vs. transactional fundraising

The culture of an organization drives its approach to fundraising. An organization's view of the donor relationship defines whether they use relationship-based or transactional (commodity-based) fundraising.

Transformational relationships

Fundraising serves philanthropy. As we mentioned earlier, fundraising is a vehicle through which society invests in its values and passions.

In a transformational relationship culture

- *The primary goal is the relationship and the value the advocate brings to the cause.*
- *The organization is a supplier of value and opportunity to the donor relationship.*
- *The donor and volunteer are significant parts of the equation for impact. Fundraising and volunteer development should be prioritized at the same level as direct program service as they are part of what makes that possible.*
- *The organization views donors and volunteers as partners.*
- *The donor is giving through the organization to realize a greater desire they have.*
- *Gifts given and received are abundant, meaningful, and long lasting.*
- *The organization moves from a mindset of scarcity to one of abundance.*
- *The organization believes the donor and volunteer are receiving true value from our exchange.*
- *Our exchange drives renewal, engagement, and sustainability.*

$$Philanthropy = \heartsuit + \text{☺}$$

Transactional Fundraising

Transactional (commodity-based) fundraising doesn't have a clear definition most likely because very few organizations would claim they subscribe to it. However, their actions, either intentional or otherwise, show many organizations practice this approach. Organizations that practice this approach either fail to identify it as such or fail to understand their approach at all.

In a transactional fundraising culture

- *The primary goal of fundraising becomes needs and funding.*
- *The organization is only a demander of resources, not a supplier of true value to the donor.*
- *The donor is viewed and treated as merely a source of funding.*
- *The organization relies on persuasion to get what the organization wants (making a gift).*
- *Funds raised in this way become token gifts and are typically short-lived and fail to build long-lasting donor connections.*
- *The organization has a need and demands it be met through urgent and crisis-driven appeals.*
- *Produces churn and burn cultures, as well as constant fiscal crises.*

Once a transformational relationship culture of philanthropy is established, an organization's key question moves from "How can I find 500 new donors?" to "How can I help our 500 current donors reach their greatest potential?" When the right questions are being asked, success is no longer limited to the traditional measures of dollars raised or total donors. Instead, success becomes defined by donor engagement, donor depth, donor perception, and donor satisfaction. This can be a significant shift for an organization. It takes time, sometimes years, to see the shift to this transformational relationship culture of philanthropy.

$$Philanthropy = \heartsuit + \text{☺}$$

Donors want to give more, but they are not going to do so until organizations give them a reason to give. If organizations view donors as checkbooks, donations will remain token gifts. This view puts nonprofits on the demand-side and there is a very limited supply of donor funding. However, if we practice relational philanthropy and understand the value we provide donors, then donors move from giving token gifts toward investing in a transcendent cause. This means both the organization and the donor can be on the supply side, providing value to one another.

When organizations begin taking on characteristics of a high-pressure salesperson, convincing donors to make a gift even if the donor is reluctant, the organization's efforts become counterproductive. This approach tends to provide short-term results. However, research and experience show there are potential harmful long-term consequences of prospects' repeated exposure to this high-pressure approach. These consequences include decay of the organization's reputation, donor fatigue, and donor disenchantment.

$$Philanthropy = \heartsuit + \text{☺}$$

Donor care: relational vs. transactional

In a relationship fundraising culture, donor care is expressed through

- *acknowledging each gift in a timely, personal, and appropriate manner.*
- *being accountable and trustworthy.*
- *helping the donor and volunteer find their greatest value in the organization.*
- *using the donor's gifts as directed.*
- *providing information on how the donor's gift impacted the mission and vision.*
- *personalized communications when possible (e.g. handwritten notes).*

In a commodity-based fundraising culture, donor care is expressed through

- *working to provide a special benefit equal to the gift.*
- *tangible benefits like VIP treatment at events or token gifts of thanks.*
- *efficient communications instead of personalized ones (e.g. pre-recorded phone-a-thon).*

Fundraising: a servant to philanthropy

We discussed in earlier sections Hank Rosso's concept that "fundraising is a servant of philanthropy."[1] I would take this idea even further and say, "fundraising simply translates and engages." Fundraising translates something we care about (e.g. cats) in a way that allows others to act on the shared value. That is fundraising's entire role.

Philanthropy = ♡ + ☺

There's no fear, guilt, coercion, begging, or deception. Where do these negative motives come from? These motives originate from asking people who hate cats to become cat lovers by playing the game of conversion. Instead, organizations should engage those who share the same cause (e.g. love of cats) with us. If I routinely ask cat haters to become cat lovers, then my lack of understanding about what these individuals care about will be taken personally. I'll become a nuisance.

However, if I'm talking to a cat lover, it's an entirely different experience. No one has ever told me, "Jamie, I do love cats and want to see your cat mission succeed, but I'm offended that you invited me to be a part of it."

Unfortunately, the typical donor experience does not include having their interests understood or engaged. The average person is often invited to give to organizations they couldn't care less about. Based on thousands of donor interviews my team and I do each year, many donors say, "The greatest thing an organization can do is realize my giving isn't about them. It's about me. It's not about what they need; it's about me being able to be a part of something that's bigger than myself. They don't get it, so what happens? I become a checkbook." The average donor relationship in the U.S. has become a simple transaction.

Shifting the organization's mindset from transactional to transformational relationships changes the entire playing field of what fundraising is about. Professionals in the field of fundraising get this. Most senior level gift officers will tell you they love their job. They see their job as rewarding.

$$Philanthropy = \heartsuit + \text{☺}$$

These senior level gifts officers get to take people who care about the same things their organization cares about and offer those individuals a way to be a part of it while discovering a value they have never experienced.

When you talk with those in fundraising who don't get it, you hear, "Fundraising is a necessary evil. I hate fundraising." This negative mindset has an impact on the profession. A national study was conducted with senior development professionals in 2012. The study found 68% of those professionals were seeking to leave their jobs. The number-one reason was leadership (the board/Executive Director/CEO) did not promote genuine development sustainability but instead focused on transactional or commodity-based fundraising approaches (2012 Chronicle of Philanthropy, Bridge span study).

The average donor has the same unfortunate perception about fundraising as the average mid-level nonprofit staff member. These donors had the experience of being invited to events they didn't care about, people continually asking them to give but not paying attention to their needs, and organizations not valuing their relationship.

When we begin to help nonprofit professionals understand how they are connecting donors to their cause, it changes how these professionals engage with fundraising. Their roles move from knocking on doors to inviting people into something bigger than themselves.

$$Philanthropy = \heartsuit + \text{☺}$$

Engaging in all three pillars

The most fulfilling thing a donor can have is a relationship with an organization that engages their abilities, giving, and passion for the cause. For many donors, that simply doesn't exist. They give to a few organizations, volunteer elsewhere, and advocate somewhere else. This happens because the relationship between the organization and the donor has not been built to experience how all three pillars can come together.

When an organization engages a donor in all three levels, the donor receives fulfillment and becomes a partner in impact. If donors are only engaged in one or two levels, this impact cannot be fully obtained.

To move to this place as an organization, we must expand our view of what each of the three pillars can include. We should not limit volunteering to formal and performance-driven tasks, not limit giving to major gifts, and not limit advocacy to the person who is vocal about our cause.

$$Philanthropy = \heartsuit + \text{☺}$$

MISSION, VISION, AND IMPACT

*The vision is
the peak of
the mountain
your entire
organization
is climbing.*

Vision and mission: the 1% rule

Vision

The vision is our ultimate destination. John D. Rockefeller had a very simple organizational philosophy. It was focused on the idea that a strong organization consisted of two critical things:

1. *A strong organization consists of 1% vision and 99% of all resources lined up behind that vision.*
2. *If you could achieve and master those two things, you could build anything.*

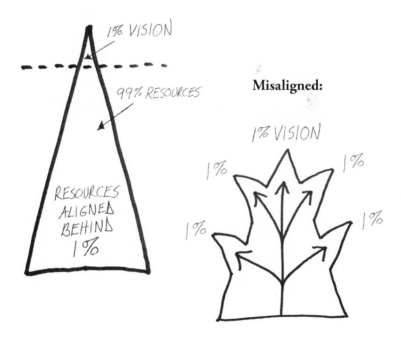

Aligned:

1% VISION

99% RESOURCES

RESOURCES
ALIGNED
BEHIND
1%

Misaligned:

1% VISION

1%   1%

1%   1%

Philanthropy = ♡ + ☺

Your organization has a variety of resources. Obviously, cash is one. Most of your resources are people (staff, volunteers, and members/participants). Other resources include facilities, equipment, strategic plan, brand, culture, and intellectual properties. All these resources need to align to that specific 1% vision.

Very few organizations achieve this level of focus. This is not simply saying, "All our money goes directly to our programs." This level of focus requires a vision so strong that it serves like a magnetic field, pulling the rest of the organization into it. It's a vision so clear that everyone who is a part of the organization knows it, understands it, communicates it, and lives it.

That tip of the pyramid is the 1% vision. The vision is the peak of the mountain your entire organization is climbing.

The unwelcomed news: it's challenging work to "sharpen" the tip of the pyramid into focus. Most people are more comfortable thinking about solving problems instead of focusing on what the ultimate impact of the work needs to be. There is a cost to an organization that does not seek to sharpen its focus. The organization's vision becomes progressively more difficult to align resources underneath.

A spear without a tip is just a big pole. The vision is what makes the organization. It's why the organization exists in the first place.

When we invest in the 99% of resources instead of the 1% of vision, the result is multiple, competing goals. Throughout the organization, different people then implement different processes to achieve different goals. The goals then often compete, and the organization moves into chaos, silos, mediocrity, or ineffectiveness.

$$Philanthropy = \heartsuit + \text{☺}$$

When we lack focus, the work of achieving our mission and vision becomes diluted. We shift from an army focused on a single, critical target to a crowd simply chasing dollars no matter the target. The organization moves from an external focus to an internal focus on the finances of the organization itself. Morale begins to break down. Teamwork, accountability, and trust decline.

The cause the organization was created for loses. Without a clear focus, the 1% pyramid turns into an unpruned evergreen tree, with multiple tips, or competing 1%'s.

Why?

It's simply much harder to focus on the 1%. We spend most of our time figuring out resources like budgets, best practices, staffing, programming, and fundraising. Yet if we don't invest in the clarity of our 1% vision, how do we know those resources are pointing in the right direction?

Fundraising also suffers from a lack of vision. There's a saying that goes, "It is the mission that gets the donor on the boat; it is the vision that keeps them there."

If we don't develop an organizational discipline and culture to define, contextualize, and focus on the 1%, we will most likely never achieve anticipated results. Ignoring the 1% vision opens the door to mediocrity. Clarity opens the door to impact. The 1% opens the door to potential.

When the vision is clear, then we can define the type of impact we should create that will address why the need exists and our vision to address it. Then we can better clarify the

Philanthropy $= \heartsuit +$

changes needed to facilitate that broader impact, define the outputs (the things we produced or delivered), and use that to drive our daily activities. This all has to be in alignment to the vision for real transformation to occur.

Vision to activities process:

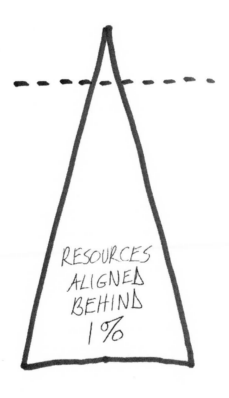

$Philanthropy = \heartsuit + \text{☺}$

Mission

People get involved with a nonprofit to make a difference. Whether donors, volunteers, or staff, individuals are first attracted to the mission. The mission is our core belief and what it is that we do to realize that core belief. The person and the organization share a core belief (e.g. cats) and the individual gets on board with the work the nonprofit is doing with that shared belief (e.g. protecting cats).

Fundraising translates how people can make a difference in a cause they care about. Simply knowing there's a need (e.g. cats are living on the street) isn't enough to attract or engage a donor. Information on a donor's potential impact (e.g. "you can put 10 cats in a home for $200") makes the difference.

Collecting and communicating results (e.g. "you helped rescue 3,247 cats this year") reminds individuals of their impact. It also allows the organization's leadership and staff to make informed decisions about which activities to engage in. If an organization's activities are aligned with the mission, there will be relevant results to collect and communicate.

Philanthropy = ♡ + ☺

Magic Minds' volunteers and donors continued to pitch great ideas to Charlie and the board. Ideas ranged from ways to improve the children's classroom experience to new programs to meeting needs that surfaced with the kids in the classroom.

One idea a large group of illusionists rallied around, after hearing some of the students received very little food at home over the weekends, was to create a Friday after-school food program. In this program, Magic Minds' classroom facilitators would collect food items throughout the week and provide a bag of nutritious food to students in need for the weekend.

While this was a wonderful idea, some countered it with the point that Magic Minds had grown so fast that the organization was barely able to provide their current services at a high enough quality. Many of the illusionists were taking on more classes than their schedule allowed, and there was a lack of time to correctly prepare.

Through many heated discussions, the question was raised, "Why does Magic Minds exist?" This led to some great discussions among everyone, from the board to volunteers.

As a result, Magic Minds crafted a mission and vision statement. The organization needed to specifically state why it existed as an organization and what its ultimate outcome was. Magic Minds began with the intent to help under-resourced children learn illusion and reap the rewards of increased people skills, learning ability, and creativity. Magic Minds discovered those were the needs their organization could uniquely meet. Magic Minds existed to teach illusion to under-resourced children with the intent of providing children the opportunity to grow in people skills, learning ability, and creativity. As an organization, Magic Minds realized there were simply too many needs in the students' lives to meet but that their organization could partner with other nonprofits to connect those children to what they needed.

Unfortunately, this led to a fallout with about a dozen volunteers and donors who were passionate about the food program. Yet clarity and vision were brought to those who remained. It also brought a level of identity and unity that had gotten lost.

An organization's mission should drive every decision about every activity. When an organization's activities are aligned to its vision, informed by its mission, and filtered through its core values, an organization is moving toward its full potential.

Philanthropy = ♡ + 🙂

DONOR RELATIONSHIP GROWTH

*You are
building
life-long
advocates.*

Our job as nonprofits is to help those who share the same values grow in their expression of what they care about. So what does that look like, and how do we get there?

We'll look at both questions together, but first let's lay the foundation.

The case for support

To help engage someone in a cause they care about, the first critical building block for a fundraising program is the case for support. This answers the question "Why care?" It connects the dots to why a potential donor should care about your cause and why they would want to support it financially.

Yes, this probably seems obvious to you. However, never make the mistake of assuming someone knows why something is important. It's your job to build a bridge to help them clearly see the need, why they should care, and why your organization is the best way for them to serve the cause.

How do you create a case for support?

To answer the question "Why care?" and craft a compelling case for support, start by answering the following questions:

1. *Why do we exist?*
2. *How do we make a better community and society?*
3. *Who am I talking to?*
4. *What are our vision and our values that will connect people to our cause?*

Philanthropy = ♡ + 🙂

While most organizations have a wide variety of supporters, each type of donor may support the cause for a different reason. Each group may also have varied worldviews, assumptions, or filters through which they view your cause and the issues surrounding it. Creating meaningful interactions might look different for each group of individuals but will go back to their connection to the cause and the shared vision and/or values.

For example, a faith-based nonprofit doing inner-city poverty work may need to connect with representatives from corporations who are not religiously affiliated, non-faith-based individuals who are passionate about their services and their outcomes. Each of these people is connecting to the same cause, but from a different angle or shared value. Therefore, they each need to be communicated with differently.

Successful fundraising depends on your ability to

1. *translate the case for support into various expressions (e.g. social media, websites, brochures, appeal letters, speeches, grant proposals, etc.),*
2. *transmit those expressions to people (potential donors) who share an interest and who are connected to your cause.*

The relationship starts with the case for support—this is the foundation of the relationship. It helps a potential donor understand if your organization is a possible match with their passion as an individual. Potential donors are presented with the opportunity to decide if they care your organization exist—does your work resonate with their passions? If you're both passionate about the same cause, the potential donor then decides if your organization is the right fit for

Philanthropy = ♡ + ☺

them to step in the boat with you. The case for support is like that first step donors take that allows them to get in the boat with you.

If cultivated well, the donor's relationship with your organization grows over time. They give regularly. They volunteer. They advocate. You help them discover ways to better serve the cause in their own unique way. They flourish as they invest their time, talents, and heart in a cause they're passionate about. Your shared vision and values grow as together you make society better.

Just as my wife and I went from "you're cute and funny" to dating to engaged to married to parents and will continue with new stages of our relationship, a donor enters new stages of their relationship with your organization.

The donor's relationship can then grow into three further phases:

1. **Primary:** *The donor is ready to explore potential shared values and vision about the programs and services your organization offers.*
2. **Intimacy:** *Donor advocacy and support of your organization moves past services and tangible aspects into advocacy and support for the heart of your organization.*
3. **Legacy:** *Donor advocacy and support move from supporting the heart of your organization to ensuring the heart will be strong for years to come.*

Let's explore these a bit further.

Philanthropy = ♡ + 🙂

Primacy

Primacy is when people have a (prime) connection to the work and cause of your organization. They share a common value with you; a common expression in helping society. They are growing in their passion for the programs and services you offer.

Primacy happens because donors have a more prime connection with your organization and the cause. Whether they visited the program first-hand, made a difference in their kids' lives, or some other reason, they resonated with something concrete and tangible. They connected to the work in a strong way.

Intimacy

The donor relationship can then potentially grow from primacy to intimacy. In primacy, the actual work of your organization (programs and services) and the shared values in that work are the glue of the relationship. In intimacy, donors move past tangible services and work to understanding the heart of the organization. They understand if you don't have the right infrastructure, capacity, and ability to pay a competitive wage, etc., the services they were first attracted to supporting cannot be sustained. They happily invest in administration, facilities, and operating expenses because they see how those affect the programs and services. They realize everything you do and everything they fund is mission focused. Each element is part of the equation for changing a life. If any element wasn't, you wouldn't spend money on it.

$$Philanthropy = \heartsuit + \text{☺}$$

Securing the heart of the organization is crucial to continue the work the organization is created to accomplish.

Legacy

Legacy moves from intimacy's working to make sure the heart is strong to making sure the heart is strong in 20 years. Donors in the legacy phase want to invest in the heart of the organization for years to come. Legacy relationships drive things like deeply sacrificial major gifts, endowment gifts, and planned giving.

If we're doing our job correctly as nonprofits, then as donors come into primacy, we educate them not only about our services, but also about the heart of the organization. We will then also educate them about the future heart of the organization.

However, if we're doing our job incorrectly, donors can get stuck at a primacy or intimacy level. Without proper cultivation, the donors will fail to see the value the heart of the organization brings to the cause they are passionate about. Our job is to help the donors have the trust and understanding to go deeper in our relationship. A donor who wants more understanding of the heart but does not receive it ends up with a limited perspective of why things matter.

A limited perspective will cause donors to answer their own questions, like "How much of your money goes to mission and programs?" in ways that are not accurate. We know that ALL funds go toward mission. Operational expenses are directly focused and aligned to further the mission. If they aren't, they shouldn't be spent.

$$Philanthropy = \heartsuit + \text{☺}$$

It is our responsibility to cultivate these relationships. If we stop the cultivation process, the donors never understand the heart of the organization. If they never understand that, we end up with poor planned-giving programs, insufficient endowment building, and weak long-term relationships. As we cultivate these relationships, we help them "see what we see" and understand more fully the bigger picture of how they can support the work they love.

Long-Term Advocates

The Salvation Army International has one of the best planned-giving programs in the country. It has been said the Vice President of Planned Giving was asked how the organization was so successful at this, when most organizations fail. His answer was simple: most organizations fail to see the donor as more than a three-year relationship. The Salvation Army, however, views each donor today as a 30-year relationship.

Three years versus 30-years is a profound difference in perspective.

What happens when you view the volunteer or donor as someone who will be with the organization in 30 years? Whether they give $1 or $1,000 per year, you're seeking to engage and develop a 30-year relationship with them. What kind of changes would you make in your organization?

You will invest more in long-term relationships.

Your job is to help donors find their greatest potential in creating impact around shared vision and values. When organizations do that, they see the blossoming of long-term advocates for the cause.

$$Philanthropy = \heartsuit + \text{☺}$$

The Salvation Army went through a major policy shift in how they operate that had an impact on their overall philosophy. As part of their process, they contacted as many donors as possible and asked them for their feedback.

I was able to talk with a donor who had an issue with the changes they made, so she wrote a letter letting them know her concerns. However, this donor had only been giving about $50 a year over the last five years. In an organization as large as the Salvation Army, she feared she would never be heard.

Within five days of her mailing the letter, she received a phone call from the international office saying, "I want to make sure we fully understand what you're seeing in this and you understand completely why this is important." They believe in 30 years this lady will inherit the decisions they are making today. It's being both donor-centered and relationship-centered. It's prioritizing stewardship over solicitation. It's moving past short-term inefficiencies into long-term relationships. The next major step is helping empower those who care to find their greatest place of impact with us.

As an example, prioritizing stewardship means things like thanking people in meaningful ways and not attaching a giving request to a thank you. The donor is saying, "If you're going to thank me, then thank me. But if you thank me and then ask me to give, is the purpose of you thanking me just an excuse to ask me to give? Or are you thanking me because I really mean something?"

Stewardship provides clarity knowing the donor will be here from year to year. It is about affirmation of the relationship. Therefore, you act in a way to build the relationship.

$$Philanthropy = \heartsuit + \text{☺}$$

From the work
to the heart
to the future.

From donors to volunteers to board members, you build relationships that enable individuals to move from primacy to intimacy to legacy. From the work to the heart to the future.

You are building life-long advocates.

Philanthropy = ♡ + 🙂

CHAPTER 8

BOARD LEADERSHIP AND PHILANTHROPY

The board is designed to consist of the most passionate and invested supporters of your cause.

The board is designed to consist of the most passionate and invested supporters of your cause. They should be a unified body of leadership focused on shared passion and vision, spurring each other on to champion and advocate a cause that is changing lives and building a better society. It is the heart of an organization structured to serve both clients and supporters through philanthropy.

Yet would many of us say this is how our board operates?

The board can easily slide from this ideal vision into a group of people simply coming to meetings. From passionate champions to commodities. From a unified group to individuals with competing agendas.

The biggest challenge

The largest barrier to a board operating at its potential is moving from a group of individuals to a unified leadership team. As referred to earlier, "culture eats strategy for lunch." What we have is a board culture issue, not a board strategy issue.

Have you ever watched an NBA all-star game? If so, you'll notice it's made up of incredibly talented stars. However, you typically won't notice great teamwork or a great team. Stars don't make teams. Coaches who build excellent teams don't look for a group of stars; they instead look for players who work to become exponentially greater together.

In much the same way, instead of being built out of passion, modern boards are often built by "star" individuals who bring image, experience, stature, or wealth to the team.

$$Philanthropy = \heartsuit + \text{(figure)}$$

Passion for the cause is reduced to a backseat passenger—if a passenger at all.

This has led to a major downfall, or even dysfunction, at the level of the board. The board is diminished to a short-term mindset and a transactional relationship rather than a 30-year relationship with someone who will become a life-long advocate for the cause, much beyond their service on the board.

Until we move from a board of "star" individuals to a true unified body of leadership, the organization will fail to realize its full potential.

The board is one of the most essential elements in the sustainability equation of a nonprofit. It will make or break the future of the organization. It sets the example and defines the growth ceiling. It can also stagnate the organization. The board accepts responsibility for the cause and the vision. The board is a body of leaders who, we hope, share a desire to love others through their organizations service to the cause.

$$Philanthropy = \heartsuit + ☺$$

THE MAGIC MINDS STORY
Taking the slower path

As the size and vision of Magic Minds grew, Charlie knew he needed to add additional board members to help handle the increasing needs. However, it was progressively difficult to find illusionists who were also organizationally minded. In Charlie's desperation, he began meeting with potential board members from local corporations.

"Hey, their companies expect them to take part on a board, they can meet on company time, they're sharp at business, and they are serious movers and shakers. I think any one of them could lead this entire thing! I know they don't know or care anything about magic, but it's about kids and we need to fill more seats on this board to reach those kids," he said.

A few months later, their board had grown from seven to fifteen members. Yet at every board meeting, Charlie found himself having to explain how magic worked, why developing a homework tutoring program didn't fit the vision, why professional props were needed instead of lower cost amateur ones, and no, they weren't going to replace magic lessons with economics lessons for kids, even if the board member would fund the entire program.

Meanwhile, the fundraising and management of the programs had moved backward instead of forward, due to the distractions new board members brought.

After much drama and hurt feelings, Charlie had to ask six of the eight new members to step down from the board.

"I may not be the smartest rabbit in the hat, but I at least know I'm not going down that path again," he told one of the founding board members. "I think I'll take the slower path and wait for someone who actually cares about magic and gets it. That was miserable!"

Alignment

A tour group from Colorado boarded a bus bound for San Antonio for a weekend of sightseeing. The two bus drivers in the front seats greeted the passengers as they entered. As they prepared to depart, the first bus driver shared the itinerary and details for their arrival in San Antonio.

A few hours later, the bus drivers switched. The second driver immediately took an exit and announced over the intercom they were now on route to Houston, not San Antonio. The passengers and other bus driver voiced their confusion and frustration.

"We paid money to visit San Antonio! Houston is nice, but it's not where we planned to go."

He replied, "I'm passionate about Houston and think you will be too. Since I'm driving, you have to follow me there."

Some passengers liked the idea of Houston, but others became angry. The other bus driver attempted to take control of the wheel, which caused the bus to hit a guard rail and crash. Everyone was safe, but no one reached their destination.

In an organization, the board members are the bus drivers.

The board is ultimately responsible for holding and leading the vision of the organization—leading it toward the correct destination. When board members do not share a collective and clear vision, they can divert the work from the intended target.

$$Philanthropy = \heartsuit + \text{☺}$$

Since board members are the most intimate volunteers, donors, and advocates, we must nourish the board, set clear expectations for them, and invest in them as an asset at the very center of the organization. Anything less degrades the core of what the board is designed to be.

$Philanthropy =$ ♡ + 🙂

ECONOMICS
OF
FUNDRAISING

Relationships trump statistics. Relationships trump efficiency. Relationships win.

DONORS REVENUES

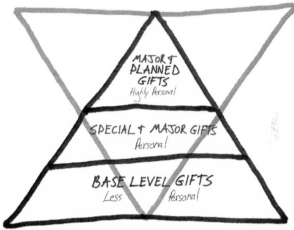

(Fundraising Pyramid adapted from The Fund Raising School Indiana University Lilly Family School of Philanthropy.)[1]

Major & Planned Gifts:
Cost average $.01 - $.10 per $1. Relationship average 8+ years. Average 60% of revenues from 10% of donors.

Special & Major Gifts:
Cost average $.25 - $1.50 per $1. Relationship average 0-3 years. Average 20% of revenues from 70% of donors.

Base Level Gifts:
Cost average $.15 - $.25 per $1. Relationship average 4-8 years. Average 20% of revenues from 20% of donors.

At first glance, the fundraising pyramid above brings about one response: only pursue major and planned gifts. Running the numbers, this makes total sense, right?

Philanthropy = ♡ + 🧍

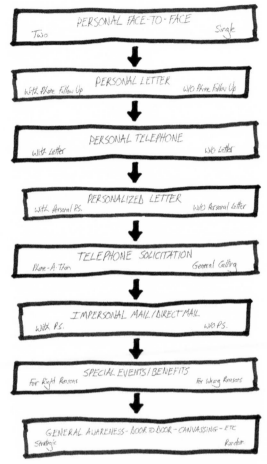

LADDER OF EFFECTIVENESS IN SOLICITATION
Most to Least, Left more effective than right side

PERSONAL FACE-TO-FACE
Two   Single

PERSONAL LETTER
With Phone Follow Up   W/O Phone Follow Up

PERSONAL TELEPHONE
With Letter   W/O Letter

PERSONALIZED LETTER
With Personal P.S.   W/O Personal Letter

TELEPHONE SOLICITATION
Phone-A-Thon   General Calling

IMPERSONAL MAIL / DIRECT MAIL
With P.S.   W/O P.S.

SPECIAL EVENTS / BENEFITS
For Right Reasons   For Wrong Reasons

GENERAL AWARENESS - DOOR TO DOOR - CANVASSING - ETC
Strategic   Random

(Ladder of Effectiveness adapted from The Fund Raising School
Indiana University Lilly Family School of Philanthropy.)[2]

When we look at the many ways we communicate with donors on this ladder of effectiveness, we come to the same conclusion, correct? Just say yes to meeting face to face with donors for major gifts.

$$Philanthropy = \heartsuit + \text{☺}$$

You may be wondering why then bother with special events, social media, direct mail, etc.? Skip ahead to the high impact, high level gifts.

Let's step back and look at this from a long-term view. Let's pretend your donors are a family. This family is dedicated to the cause of cats. The major and planned gift donors are the grandparents and great-grandparents. They've earned and saved enough to invest significantly toward cats.

If you're a strategic development professional, you simply target those grandparents and great-grandparents. It's a great plan—if you plan on closing your doors in a few years.

Not to be crass, but grandparents and great-grandparents pass away. Once they're gone, who is going to pick up where they left off? The cause will stagnate, and no one will be left to advocate for the cats. You neglected to cultivate a relationship with the parents and children, and those individuals decided to give to a different cat-loving organization. There is no generational impact, just one generation.

A long-term approach to fundraising realizes donor relationships need to be cultivated at every age and every stage of the relationship. In the short-term, that may result in higher expenses for the organization to connect with some donors. Yet just like the Salvation Army example earlier, let's think in a 30-year term, not three.

You are building a river of relationships that will continue to flow and power the work of your cause for years to come. Those relationships come from a variety of streams and result in a variety of outcomes.

When we simply measure our fundraising efforts on a specific

$$Philanthropy = \heartsuit + \text{☺}$$

campaign or year, we can accidentally sabotage long-term results. When we measure success by money and not by our ability to mobilize advocates around our shared values and vision, we reduce those who care to checkbooks.

Giving level isn't the only evidence of the relationship

We often simply associate the dollar amount of a gift to the depth of someone's relationship to the cause. Yes, giving level is one indicator. But giving level by itself doesn't tell us much at all. We interview donors who give $15,000 a year to one organization and $500,000 a year to another, and the $15,000 organization believes they are one of their closest donors. However, that donor tells us the $15,000 is a token gift because there is no real relationship.

What about the donor who gives $25 most years, gives $75 other years, but does it for 12 years straight? In most organizations, this donor would be a low priority. Their relationship wouldn't be valued.

There is story after story of the donor who gave small amounts for years, then made a mega gift later down the road. We have all heard them, and I have worked with those donors and seen this happen many, many times.

One couple had a son who visited a seminary with intentions to attend. The son eventually changed his plans, but the parents fell in love with the seminary. Every year they would go down for three or four days to visit. They referred individuals to the school but never gave any gifts to the school. When the couple could no longer drive themselves, the seminary sent a priest over seven hours to

Philanthropy = ♡ + ☺

pick them up to continue their tradition of visiting annually, then would drive them back home.

This couple never gave any gifts. They weren't classified as "wealthy" or prestigious prospects. They were simply advocates who fell in love with the seminary.

The seminary valued their relationship. Every year they ensured the couple was able to visit the seminary, even if that meant driving to pick them up. After the couple passed away, they left the seminary $22 million. Why? Because they were advocates of a shared passion, shared value, and shared vision.

Ratios, stats, and our efforts in the field are all very important, but they are not the complete picture. Relationships trump statistics. Relationships trump efficiency. Relationships win.

We must never minimize a relationship, because there are no minimal people. Instead, we must seek to build relationships with people who are passionate about the cause. There will always be those who give out of goodwill, but our focus must be on finding individuals with shared values and vision around our common passion. Those who give out of goodwill will still give, but those who give out of shared passion will go somewhere else if there is not a relationship.

$$Philanthropy = \heartsuit + \text{(stick figure)}$$

ACHIEVING PHILANTHROPIC SUSTAINABILITY

Donors want to give and want to know how to give because they care about the cause.

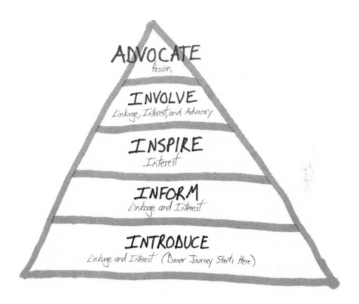

Potential supporters become first-time donors by introducing them to and informing them about your cause, work, and organization. They connect by being linked, interested, or both. This is the foundation of cultivating donor relationships. However, they do not have to stay at the base forever. They might leave the organization altogether (attrition rates for first-time donors can be as high as 60-80%). They can also deepen their relationship with the organization.

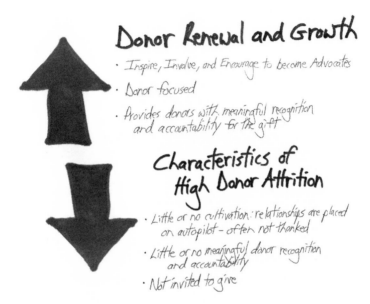

Donor Renewal and Growth

- Inspire, Involve, and Encourage to become Advocates
- Donor focused
- Provides donors with meaningful recognition and accountability for the gift

Characteristics of High Donor Attrition

- Little or no cultivation: relationships are placed on autopilot - often not thanked
- Little or no meaningful donor recognition and accountability
- Not invited to give

Nonprofits can cultivate relationships and more deeply connect donors and volunteers to the cause by

1. *inspiring* them to be a part of something bigger than themselves.
2. *involving* them with the organization by volunteering.
3. *advocating* for the organization and its cause.

$$Philanthropy = \heartsuit + \text{♀}$$

The key for getting donors involved and helping them grow into advocates is to engage them and listen. Here are some powerful questions to help strengthen their relationship to the cause:

- *Why do you give to our organization?*
- *How does our cause connect with your life and your passions?*
- *How can we learn from what you see in the cause we are both part of?*
- *Do you feel appreciated by our organization?*
- *Do you want to get involved further?*
- *Do you know how you want to get involved?*
- *How satisfied are you with your relationship to our organization?*
- *How can we improve our relationship with you?*
- *What are you passionate about?*

If you focus on the lifetime value of a donor relationship, for every 10% improvement your organization has in retaining current donors, you can double the lifetime giving value of your current donor base. Think about the implications.

The greatest key to retaining a donor is to create a meaningful relationship with each donor and serve them by inspiring them, involving them, and encouraging them to become an advocate. This meaningful relationship will naturally create discussion around a topic if or when an issue arises. Rather than simply leaving, donors will voice their concern and work with you to come to an agreement. They will do this because they care about both the cause and your organization. They are a part of it. They have a relationship with you.

Without that relationship, if they are frustrated, they simply walk away. If supporters are not connected strongly enough to the organization or do not have enough trust in the relationship, they will not voice their concerns. They're not invested relationally.

$$Philanthropy = \heartsuit + \text{👤}$$

The core function of the sustainable fundraising program

What is the core function of a sustainable fundraising program? To equip and mobilize advocates for the cause. This means caring for those who share our vision and our values. Donor care is learning enough to build trust in relationships and, therefore, knowing how to equip donors as advocates. These advocates then carry the cause forward.

Philanthropy = ♡ + 👤

Bill was a Magic Minds board member for five years. He loved the cause and loved being a part of the organization. However, during the fifth year Bill's daughter became ill, which required Bill to step off the board to care for her. Charlie understandably didn't want to burden Bill with any further commitments, so he didn't contact him much during that time.

Bill told Charlie just before stepping off the board that he couldn't really see himself serving on a board anymore, even if his daughter's circumstances changed. He was hoping to retire in the next couple of years. He wanted to have more flexibility and fewer time commitments.

Charlie thought, "I appreciate that he served five years on our board, so I guess he's done with Magic Minds. He had a good run."

Two years later, his daughter recovered, and Bill was able to go back to work. Unfortunately, Charlie had almost no contact with Bill that last year. He didn't realize Bill was still passionate about serving kids through Magic Minds. He also didn't know Bill was wanting to get involved in something again.

In the meantime, Bill had been approached by another organization that tutors kids through an after-school program. Since Charlie had not continued cultivating his relationship with Bill, Bill didn't feel connected to Magic Minds anymore. Bill thought the new organization seemed to be a good fit and that the timing was right, so he jumped in and began serving and giving there.

Bill would have been happy to get involved with Magic Minds again, just not at a board level. However, the lack of continued relationship disconnected Bill from getting involved.

Donor care simply means investing in the relationship. With the investment, there are three main components to donor care that create a healthy, sustainable relationship that grows over time.

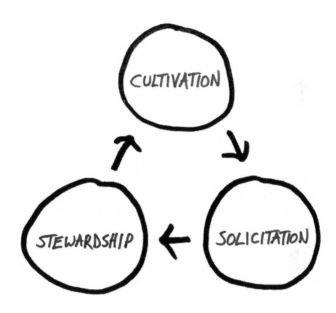

$Philanthropy =$ ♡ + 👤

Donor care: cultivation (learning)

Cultivation boils down to learning about the people who share your cause's vision and values while fostering genuine trust in the relationship. Caring about them naturally leads to a relationship instead of a mere transaction. It's an attitude of "You're here because we share this same vision and we want to continue to share it together." This relationship and concern for the donor is fed by mutual communication. Not just mass communication, but interpersonal communication. It means prioritizing face-to-face meetings, personal phone calls, personal emails, and handwritten notes as much as your organization's resources allow. It means we prioritize listening to the donor and volunteer. Learning from them how they relate to our cause, what their relationship with our cause is, and what impact through us looks like to them. Asking them to share what their legacy is and how we can help fulfill that. If we don't understand our donors' dreams, we can never help them fulfill them in our shared calling.

In these communications, it also means making the supporter the "main character" of the story instead of you. It's not saying, "Our organization is the hero; look at all the wonderful things we did." Instead, it's saying, "Look at what we did together!"

When donors are pursued as someone to serve and provide value to instead of pursued simply for money, the organization can be transformed. This new dynamic of exchanged value creates the potential for lasting and sustainable relationships.

$$Philanthropy = \heartsuit + \text{☺}$$

Donor care: solicitation (inviting)

To authentically build relationships like this, nonprofits need to come to a point of realizing a donor's investment is not because of their convincing, coercing, or obligating someone to do something. If they are a cat lover, they're here because they truly love cats. They're not here because someone tried to convert a dog lover into a cat lover. Nonprofits simply give individuals opportunities to engage in what they care about—a way to invest in their values.

If we're operating out of this philanthropic mindset, then solicitation—inviting someone to give—is part of donor care. Why? Because it's allowing donors to engage in what they care about. It's honestly and transparently letting them know what the needs of the organization are. It is about sharing with them how they can help. It is about partnering with them to find their place of the greatest potential for impact within the organization and for the cause. If we don't invite them, they may miss out on an opportunity to be enriched through a deeper connection with our shared vision and values.

My company surveys 4,000 to 8,000 donors a year. One question we ask is, "What are your needs?" More than half of these donors say, "I want more clear information on what the need is, how I can be a part of helping, and what urgent situations are needing to be addressed."

Donors want to give and want to know how to give because they care about the cause. You're allowing someone who loves cats to know the cats being served have a need. Since those cats can't speak for themselves, your organization stands in the gap and connects cat lovers to cats. You're helping donors achieve their philanthropic goals.

$$Philanthropy = \heartsuit + \text{👤}$$

Donor care: stewardship (affirming)

To grow and sustain these relationships, we must steward them by affirming the donor and volunteer relationship in meaningful and personal ways. Stewardship is affirming these relationships through ways that help donors see what they are a part of. This is expressed by thanking them for their involvement through the things mentioned in cultivation: face-to-face meetings, personal phone calls, personal emails, and handwritten notes. It's showing we truly care about them as individuals, not as commodities.

Statistics back this up. The average return for every $1 invested in a face-to-face invitation is $24, with an average of 83% of face-to-face solicitations ending in yes. Research from "Donor Center Fundraising" showed donors who received a personal phone call after their gift from a member of the board, gave on average 39% more the next year.[1]

However, it's not a formula. Showing appreciation in a meaningful way looks different for each donor and volunteer. Some want to meet with the Executive Director or Board Chair. Others may want an award ceremony. Some may prefer a phone call or handwritten thank you. As you develop these relationships, you discover what is most meaningful to each person, just as you would in a relationship with a close friend or family member.

The other aspect of affirming a donor or volunteer's investment is to inform them how their gifts and time are making a difference in the cause they care about. In the same way you discover the best ways to show appreciation, nonprofits can explore and find the most effective ways to show impact and accountability for a donor's gifts and a volunteer's time.

$$Philanthropy = \heartsuit + \text{👤}$$

Here are some practical tips for good donor stewardship:

- *Thank the donor within one to two days after the gift is given.*
- *Thank prospects who decline to donate after a face-to-face meeting with a personalized letter.*
- *Thank the donor at least seven times a year through the year.*
- *Show appreciation in a meaningful way.*
- *Inform donors how their gifts were used to advance the cause they care about.*
- *Build a partnership with the donor and the volunteer, engaging them as an asset for making a difference.*

Donor care needs to lead to building advocates for the cause. These advocates take the cause forward into their spheres of influence. When that is happening, others are growing in awareness and then connecting to both your cause and organization. A supporter who has a heart for the cause and is cared for properly can naturally move into an advocate for the cause and organization.

LONG-TERM THINKING

Short-term thinking yields short-term results. Long-term thinking leads to sustainability.

If you attend an Ivy League school, the school is not concerned whether your kids might come to their college. They are not trying to cultivate you as a student so that your kids will attend. They're focused on something more long-term: grandkids and great-grandkids.

Why? In these schools, the idea of brotherhood, sisterhood, and generational value is of highest importance. You are part of an intimate family as soon as you walk on campus. If you attend an Ivy League school, they're confident your kids will also attend. They're concerned about grandkids and great-grandkids. They believe when you're 80, your grandkids could be attending their school. Their perspective is your values will transfer down through the family tree. Third and fourth generation family members of someone who started a philanthropic relationship with an organization, like these schools, are not giving out of guilt or compulsion. They are giving because the values of the organization are ingrained in who they are. The organization is simply a part of their value system.

When we look at donors as a life-long relationship, we can begin thinking about what the relationship looks like at various stages of the donor's life. We can also, like Ivy League schools, look even further to the children and grandchildren of donors and discuss how we can begin to cultivate the values their family shares with our organization.

Our experiences as children, teenagers, and young adults shape our philanthropic behavior as adults. Our experiences as adults then affect our giving in our later years. Your organization intersects each person at some point in a 90-year continuum of their life. When we realize we're impacting

$$Philanthropy = \heartsuit + \text{☺}$$

people at different phases of their lives, we can then begin to understand it's our job to discover how to impact the next phase, and how to create a continuum of continuous impact.

Phases of life determine capacity to give *at that moment*, but not over the course of a lifetime. A parent saving for college tuition may not have the capacity to give large gifts even if they wanted to. However, 10 years later may be a different story. **The donor's phase of life doesn't minimize their potential. It just changes the timing.**

If we want our organizations to be sustainable and thriving 30, 60, 90 years from now, cultivation of families, children, and grandchildren is key. Short-term thinking yields short-term results. Long-term thinking leads to sustainability.

Philanthropy = ♡ + 👤

TRANSFORMING YOUR ORGANIZATION

If your cause is worth fighting for, it's worth loving for.

True philanthropy is

- *the key to your organization's success.*
- *intimate and relational.*
- *transformational.*

If your cause is worth fighting for, it's worth loving for

Building and cultivating authentic relationships with people who share a passion for your cause creates engagement and a culture of shared values and vision. This culture sustains your organization. It connects people. It helps people freely give of their resources, time, and heart.

This culture is not one that uses or burns people out. It doesn't twist arms or rely on high-pressure tactics. It doesn't try to convince a dog lover to become a cat lover.

It's a self-sustaining, renewing relationship that allows people to engage with a cause they love. It's not a token relationship with a transactional goal. It's an authentic relationship that provides value to both parties. The organization receives the value of a donor, volunteer, and/or advocate. The supporter receives the value of having an outlet or "vehicle" to express their love for people in meaningful ways—through a cause they care about.

It creates a place in which people are valued and they are loved. People are created in the image of God, and God is love. Nonprofits are simply connectors allowing people to express that love. They form a great tapestry of opportunity. In a tapestry, multiple individual threads are woven together

Philanthropy = ♡ + 👤

to create something greater than its individual parts. In the same way, nonprofits provide multiple individuals opportunities to play a part, discover their potential and calling, and make an impact in something greater than themselves.

When nonprofits realize their role in philanthropy (connecting people to the cause) and understand their role in connecting (building authentic relationships), over time people can engage with causes in deeply personal and meaningful ways.

Philanthropy is expressing our God-given calling to love people.

**If your cause is worth fighting for,
it's worth creating a thriving organization for**

Organizations are simply groups of people dedicated to a specific cause. Whether creating a profit, discovering a cure for cancer, or loving cats, the cause creates the unique purpose and vision of the organization. An organization without a vision, which exists merely to sustain itself, is not worth fighting for, will not thrive, and will ultimately implode.

A clear vision provides the rallying point for people to engage with the organization. It gives the direction and the destination for people to "hop on the bus."

Philanthropy = ♡ + ☺

To create impact and influence change for the cause, the organization needs to be led by a unified leadership team that cares deeply about the cause. The potential of the organization, which means the true potential they hold to create change for their cause, resides in leadership's ability to

- *clearly define and refine the vision of the organization.*
- *clearly, compellingly, and personally communicate the need, vision, impact, and opportunities to get involved to potential supporters.*
- *build and cultivate authentic relationships that provide value to both sides—with people who care about the cause.*

When an organization leads in the ways below, it is settling for something less than the organization was created for:

- *sustaining the entity financially instead of sustaining movement toward the cause.*
- *communicating through guilt or coercion.*
- *transactional or commodity-based fundraising.*

When the organization settles, its cause will ultimately suffer by a decrease in trust, engagement, and an eventual slide into decay of the organization. The cause suffers because the organization is no longer effectively facilitating engagement, movement, or action for the sake of the cause. It becomes busy doing work that doesn't create transformation and renewal. It is busy talking about cats but not doing any work to care for them. No change is taking place.

Philanthropy = ♡ + ☺

This does not mean those who were passionate about the cause and engaged with the organization stopped their passion for the cause. Their heart doesn't change. The organization they choose to engage with does. They will simply find another organization to express their shared values and vision through.

The reality is many organizations fall prey to the entropy that causes these problems. Without intentional, unified, and relational leadership, an organization will fail to achieve its true potential.

On the flip side, what if your organization discovers and steps into its true potential through a healthy culture of true philanthropy? What could happen in three years, 10 years, or 30 years for the cause you're working on? You may not even be able to imagine the potential impact of your organization that's waiting to be discovered as you move from doing good stuff to creating a movement that transforms lives, communities, and countries.

Shepherd Community Center embodies the transformation that takes place when a culture of true philanthropy is created. The story of this small inner-city organization in Indianapolis, Indiana, began as a typical nonprofit. Shepherd struggled to raise sufficient funds and develop and mobilize true advocates. However, our client's story began to change as the organization shifted its focus in a greater capacity to the heart of philanthropy, equipping and mobilizing advocates with a shared calling.

The organization began practicing many of the principles we talked about in this book—from engaging individuals on how to love their high-risk neighborhoods to viewing

$$Philanthropy = \heartsuit + \text{👤}$$

their supporters as life-long advocates. Even today as Shepherd continues to build a family of advocates connected by a common calling, the organization is challenging the norms in its agency and city. Not only is Shepherd doing this with those who share in its faith, but Shepherd is effectively mobilizing those who are at odds with its faith but in love with its calling.

As donors and volunteers connect to the cause, Shepherd has grown to one of the largest Indianapolis inner-city service organizations and has been featured nationally for its impact. Shepherd Community Center is transforming an entire city, and by extension many other places around the country. This didn't happen because they are exceptional people (though they are); Shepherd Community Center simply took the principles of philanthropy to heart and put them into practice. The results followed.

They are creating change.

$$Philanthropy = \heartsuit + \text{☺}$$

What do you dream about changing?

What could change look like for the cause you're working on?

- *Could it be less crime?*
- *Better education?*
- *Spiritual maturity?*
- *Healthier families?*
- *Less poverty?*
- *More understanding?*

If these things are happening, what positive ripple effects could they indirectly cause?

- *Could it be less divorce?*
- *Lack of abuse?*
- *Emotionally healthy children and grandchildren?*
- *Less racism?*
- *More love?*

These are the things you are working for. The things you are called to do. The things your organization is created to change. These are the things we fight for.

Therefore, pursue them with excellence. Pursue them with focus. Pursue them with love.

True philanthropy can change the world.

Philanthropy = ♡ + ☺

THE MAGIC MINDS STORY
Epilogue

While Charlie and the Magic Minds team made plenty of mistakes as they shared illusion with under-resourced children, they learned from those mistakes and continued to improve. They gradually and organically created an organization built upon fostering relationships through providing value to both clients and supporters.

No "magic tricks," just focused effort by a like-minded army of illusionists aimed at a clear vision.

The uniqueness of their mission attracted the attention of both local media and the illusion industry. They were featured in trade publications and soon received calls by other illusionists from around the nation wanting to start something similar in their communities.

"I can't believe my simple vision to teach magic tricks to children would achieve the impact it did," confessed Charlie. "I guess no one knows the potential their team has that's simply waiting to be discovered."

INDEX

Chapter 1: The Charitable Sector

1. "Quick Facts About Nonprofits." *Quick Facts About Nonprofits | NCCS*, nccs.urban.org/data-statistics/quick-facts-about-nonprofits.

2. "Your Guide To Intelligent Giving." *Charity Navigator,* www.charitynavigator.org/index.cfm?bay=content.view.

3. Brice McKeever and Marcus Gaddy. "The Nonprofit Workforce: By the Numbers." *Non Profit News | Nonprofit Quarterly*, 13 Jan. 2017, nonprofitquarterly.org/2016/10/24/nonprofit-workforce-numbers/.

4. Trattner, Walter I. *From Poor Law to Welfare State*. 6th ed., Simon & Schuster, Incorporated, 2018, p. 92.

5. "The Value of Volunteer Time." *Independent Sector,* independentsector.org/resource/the-value-of-volunteer-time/.

6. "Economic Impacts of 2010 Foundation Grantmaking on the U.S. Economy." *The Philanthropic Collaborative: Economic Impacts of 2010 Foundation Grantmaking on the U.S. Economy,* www.philanthropycollaborative.org/economicimpacts/.

7. "Charitable Giving & Life Satisfaction: Does Gender Matter?" *Women Give*, Lilly Family School of Philanthropy, 2017, philanthropy.iupui. edu/institutes/womens-philanthropy-institute/research/women-give.html.

8. Brown, Stephanie L. *An Altruistic Reanalysis of the Social Support Hypothesis: The Health Benefits of "Giving."* Institute for Social Research. The University of Michigan.

Chapter 2: What Is Philanthropy?

1. Gallup, Inc. "Most Americans Practice Charitable Giving, Volunteerism." *Gallup.com*, 13 Dec. 2013, news.gallup.com/poll/166250/americans-practice-charitable-giving-volunteerism.aspx.

2. Warner, Judith. "The Charitable-Giving Divide." *Www.nytimes.com*, The New York Times Magazine, 22 Aug. 2010, www.nytimes.com/2010/08/22/magazine/22FOB-wwln-t.html.

3. *The Holy Bible: New International Version*. Zondervan, 2009.

$$Philanthropy = \heartsuit + \text{\Large\Lightning}$$

Chapter 4: The Three Pillars

1. "National Center for Charitable Statistics | NCCS." *National Center for Charitable Statistics | NCCS*, nccs.urban.org/data-statistics/quick-facts-about-nonprofits

2. Giving USA 2017 | Total Charitable Donations Rise to New High of $390.05 Billion | Giving USA, givingusa.org/giving-usa-2017-total-charitable-donations-rise-to-new-high-of-390-05-billion/.

3. "Giving Statistics." *Charity Navigator*, 14 June 2017, www.charitynavigator.org/index.cfm?bay=content.view&cpid=42%statistics%2Fquick-facts-about-nonprofits.

4. Daniels, Alex. "As Wealthy Give Smaller Share of Income to Charity, Middle Class Digs Deeper." *The Chronicle of Philanthropy*, The Chronicle of Philanthropy, 6 Oct. 2014, www.philanthropy.com/article/As-Wealthy-Give-Smaller-Share/152481

5. "Study: Poor Are More Charitable Than The Wealthy." *NPR*, NPR, 8 Aug. 2010, www.npr.org/templates/story/story.php?storyId=129068241

6. Lapp, David. "The Generous Poor." *Institute for Family Studies,* ifstudies.org/blog/the-generous-poor.

7. "Giving USA | A public service initiative of the Giving Institute." *Giving USA | A public service initiative of the Giving Institute,* givingusa.org/.

8. "Charitable Giving & Life Satisfaction: Does Gender Matter?" *Women Give,* Lilly Family School of Philanthropy, 2017, philanthropy.iupui.edu/institutes/womens-philanthropy-institute/research/women-give.html.

9. Gallup, Inc. "Most Americans Practice Charitable Giving, Volunteerism." Gallup.com, 13 Dec. 2013, news.gallup.com/poll/166250/americans-practice-charitable-giving-volunteerism.aspx.

Chapter 5: A Culture of Philanthropy

1. Rosso, Henry. *Achieving Excellence in Fundraising*. Jossey-Bass, 1991.

Chapter 9: Economics of Fundraising

1. Indiana University, The Fund Raising School. *Fundraising Pyramid.* Lilly Family School of Philanthropy, Indianapolis, Indiana.

2. Indiana University, The Fund Raising School. *Ladder of Effectiveness.* Lilly Family School of Philanthropy, Indianapolis, Indiana.

Chapter 10: Achieving Philanthropic Sustainability

1. Burk, Penelope. *Donor Centered Fundraising.* Cygnus Applied Research, 2003.

Philanthropy = ♡ + 🙂

Jamie works as President and Director of Vision for JDLevy & Associates, a consulting firm dedicated to helping organizations devoted to doing good reach their true potential. Jamie, his wife, and three children live in Jasper, Indiana.

JDLevy & Associates' services focus on four key areas:
- *Vision*
- *Culture*
- *Impact*
- *Sustainability*

Learn more at jdlevyassociates.com.